DENNA BOK TILLHÖR:

This book belongs to:

_____

BJÖRN

BEAR

LODJUR

LYNX

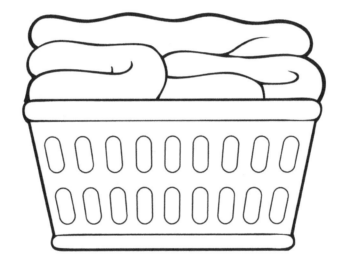

TVÄTT
LAUNDRY

BEBIS

BABY

BARNVAGN
BUGGY / STROLLER

VIKINGAR

VIKINGS

BIL CAR

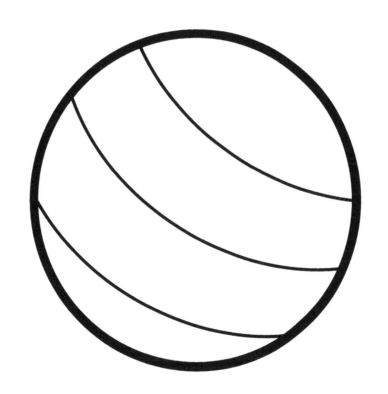

BOLL BALL

ROBOT

ROBOT

DINOSAURIE

DINOSAUR

SEGELBÅT

SAILBOAT

KÄLKE

SLEDGE

SKRIDSKOR
SKATES

SJÖRÖVARE PIRATE

PRINSESSA PRINCESS

SLOTT
CASTLE

KÄNGURU

KANGAROO

KATT

CAT

PAPEGOJA
PARROT

HUND

DOG

TRÄD TREE

RÄV
FOX

SKUNK

SKUNK

LÖV

LEAF

GRIS
PIG

FÅR

SHEEP

KO

COW

FOTBOLL
FOOTBALL/SOCCER

KALKON
TURKEY

TRAKTOR

TRACTOR

TRUMMA
DRUM

DRAGSPEL
ACCORDION

GITARR

GUITAR

BRANDMÄN*

FIRE FIGHTERS

* also 'brandbekämpare'

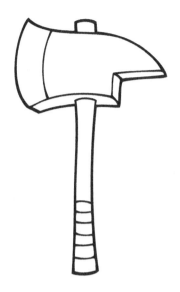

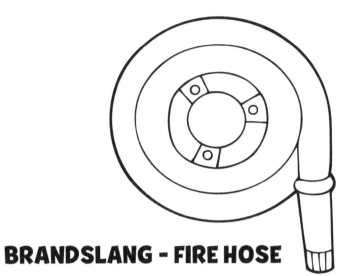

BRANDSLANG - FIRE HOSE

YXA - AXE

HJÄLM - HELMET

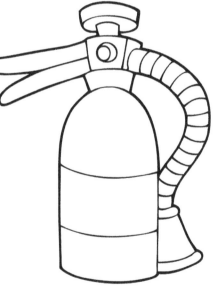

STÖVLAR - BOOTS

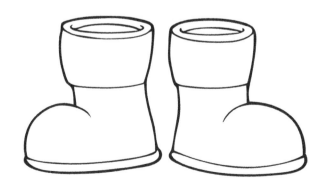

**BRANDSLÄCKARE -
FIRE EXTINGUISHER**

MAN

MAN

KVINNA
WOMAN

FLICKA - GIRL

POJKE - BOY

BARN
CHILDREN

PAPPA - DAD

MAMMA -MUM

FAMILJ
FAMILY

FLYGPLAN

AEROPLANE-AIRPLANE

ENHÖRNING

UNICORN

PARAPLY - UMBRELLA

HALSDUK - SCARF

REGNJACKA - RAIN COAT

GUMMISTÖVLAR -
WELLINGTON BOOTS
RUBBER BOOTS

VATTENPÖL - WATER PUDDLE

FJÄRIL

BUTTERFLY

SNIGEL

SNAIL

SKALBAGGE

BEETLE

BRÖDROST - TOASTER

TEKANNA - TEAPOT

TEKOPP - TEA CUP

SKRUVMEJSEL - SCREWDRIVER

SÅG - SAW

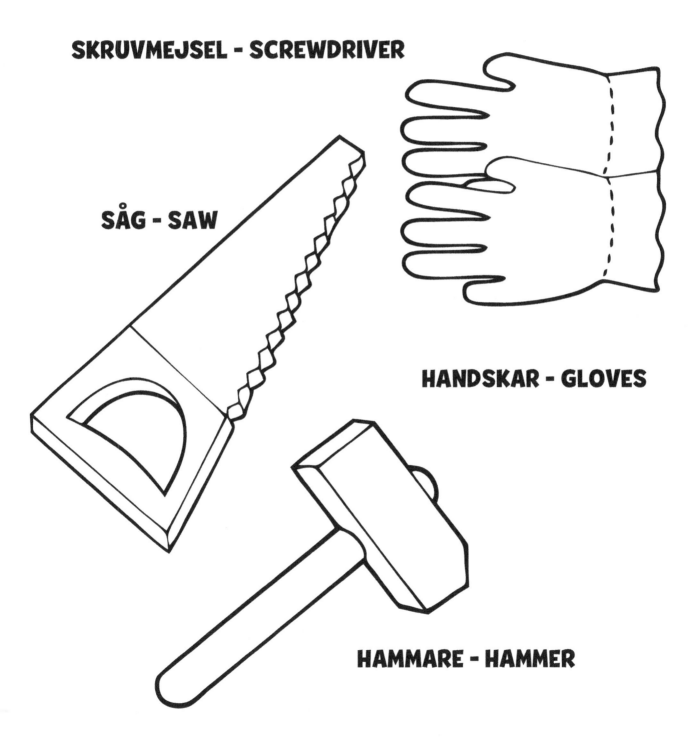

HANDSKAR - GLOVES

HAMMARE - HAMMER

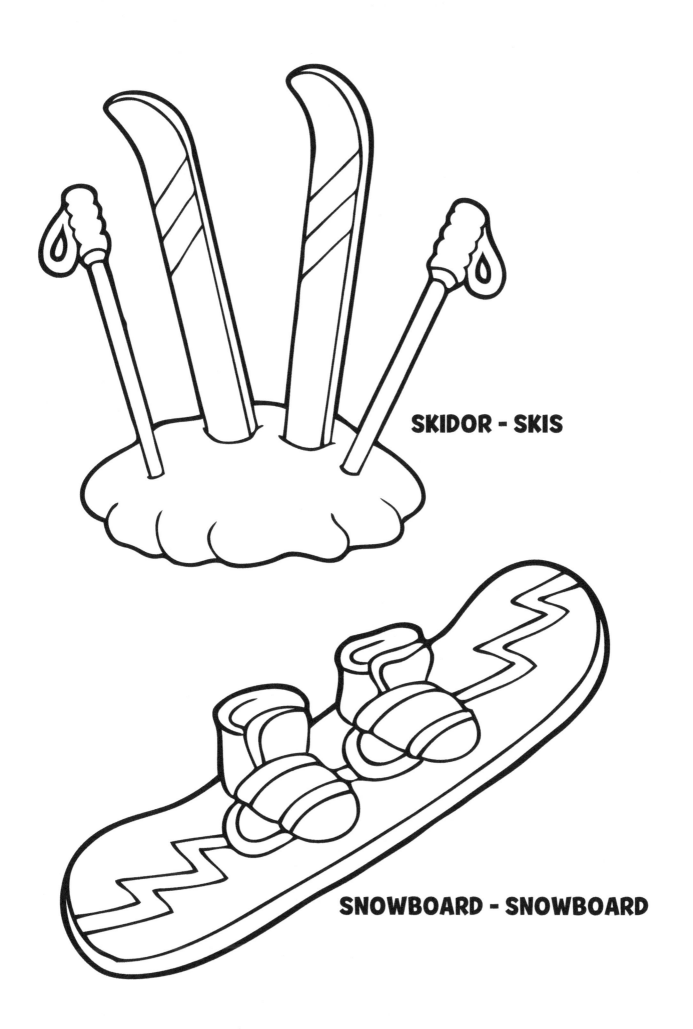

SKIDOR - SKIS

SNOWBOARD - SNOWBOARD

BADDRÄKT

SWIMSUIT

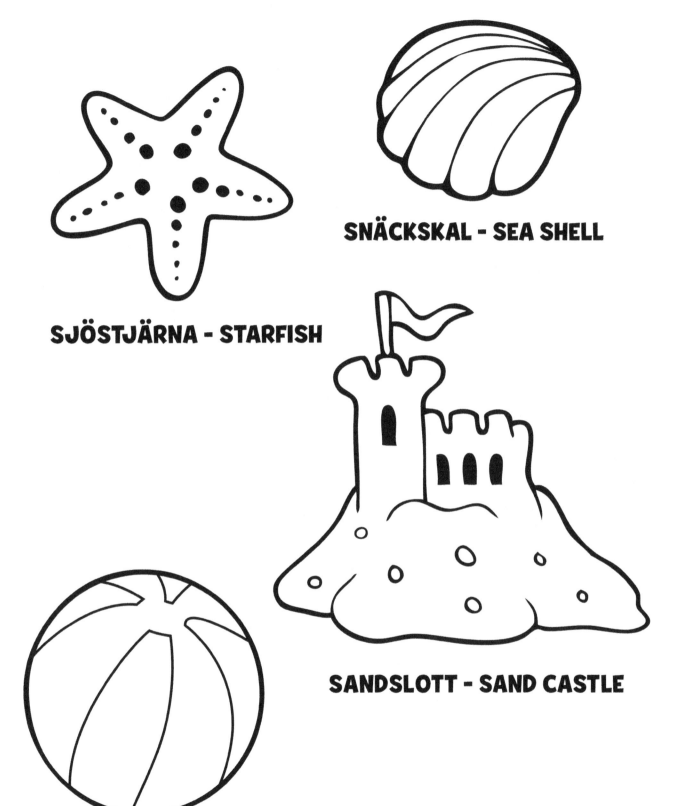

SNÄCKSKAL - SEA SHELL

SJÖSTJÄRNA - STARFISH

SANDSLOTT - SAND CASTLE

BADBOLL - BEACH BALL

JORDGUBBE - STRAWBERRY

VATTENMELON - WATER MELON

ÄPPLE - APPLE

PÄRON - PEAR

CITRON - LEMON

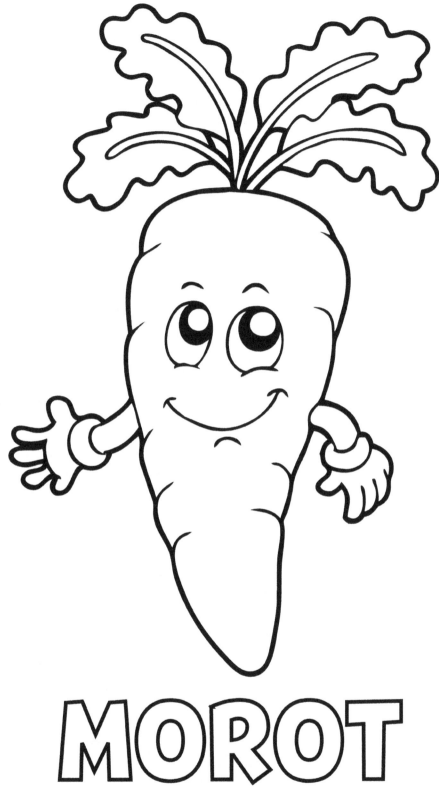

MOROT

CARROT

LÖK

ONION

Want More Pages to Color?

Ask a grown up to visit my website to buy and download your print at home coloring books, or get them as paperbacks from your favourite online bookseller.

Discover the Coloring Sweden series of fun bilingual coloring books:

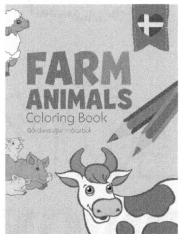

**Visit www.swenglish.life
to find your next coloring book**

Who made this book?

Hejsan! [Hello!] My name is Linda Liebrand, and I'm a Swedish mum and author living in the UK with my Dutch husband, our bouncy little boy and Swiss dog.

As you can tell, we're an international bunch and I started teaching our little boy Swedish when he was about two years old.

I write bilingual children's books specially developed for kids who learn Swedish abroad, so they can improve their vocabulary and connect with their roots.

Ask a grown up to visit my website and try one of my bilingual books for free:

www.swenglish.life/starter-library

More bilingual books:

Copyright © Linda Liebrand 2020

Paperback ISBN 978-1-913382-11-7

Published by Treetop Media Ltd 2020

Image credits:
All images by ©Klara Viskova via Shutterstock

Made in the USA
Coppell, TX
19 December 2020

46558307R00063